source to resource

FROM
RAINDROP
TAP
TO

MICHAEL BRIGHT

Crabtree Publishing Company
.com

Crabtree Publishing Company
www.crabtreebooks.com
1-800-387-7650

Published in Canada
Crabtree Publishing
616 Welland Avenue
St. Catharines, ON
L2M 5V6

Published in the United States
Crabtree Publishing
PMB 59051
350 Fifth Ave, 59th Floor
New York, NY 10118

Author: Michael Bright

Editorial director: Kathy Middleton

Freelance editor: Katie Woolley

Editors: Annabel Stones, Liza Miller, and Ellen Rodger

Designer: Rocket Design Ltd

Proofreader: Wendy Scavuzzo

Prepress technician: Samara Parent

Print and production coordinator: Katherine Berti

Published by Crabtree Publishing Company in 2017

Photographs:
p 4: NASA; p 11 (bottom): Jonathan Renouf / Alamy;
p 12 (top): Dave Blackey / All Canada Photos / Corbis;
p 15 (bottom): Jason Friend / Loop Images / Corbis;
p 18: Pratchaya Leelapatchayanont / Dreamstime;
p 19 (bottom): Typhoonski / Dreamstime;
p 21 (top): Kevin Wilton / Eye Ubiquitous / Corbis.

All other images and graphic elements courtesy of Shutterstock

Illustrations:
Stefan Chabluk: p 8; p 9; p 11 (top); p 17; p 30

First published in 2016 by Wayland
(A division of Hachette Children's Books)
Copyright © Wayland, 2016

Printed in Canada/072016/PB20160525

Every effort has been made to clear copyright. Should there be any inadvertent omission, please apply to the publisher for rectification.

The website addresses (URLs) included in this book were valid at the time of going to press. However, it is possible that contents or addresses may have changed since the publication of this book. No responsibility for any such changes can be accepted by either the author or the publisher.

Library and Archives Canada Cataloguing in Publication

Bright, Michael, author
    From raindrop to tap / Michael Bright.

(Source to resource)
Includes index.
Issued in print and electronic formats.
ISBN 978-0-7787-2708-8 (hardback).--
ISBN 978-0-7787-2712-5 (paperback).--
ISBN 978-1-4271-1818-9 (html)

    1. Water-supply--Juvenile literature. 2. Water use--Juvenile literature. 3. Hydrologic cycle--Juvenile literature. 4. Water utilities--Juvenile literature. I. Title.

TD348.B75 2016   j333.91   C2016-902595-0
                                         C2016-902596-9

Library of Congress Cataloging-in-Publication Data

Names: Bright, Michael, author.
Title: From raindrop to tap / Michael Bright.
Description: New York : Crabtree Pub. Company, 2016. | Series: Source to resource | Includes index.
Identifiers: LCCN 2016016754 (print) | LCCN 2016023072 (ebook) | ISBN 9780778727088 (reinforced library binding) | ISBN 9780778727125 (pbk.) | ISBN 9781427118189 (electronic HTML)
Subjects: LCSH: Water-supply--Juvenile literature. | Water consumption--Juvenile literature.
Classification: LCC HD1691 .B666 2016 (print) | LCC HD1691 (ebook) | DDC 333.91--dc23
LC record available at https://lccn.loc.gov/2016016754

Contents

The blue planet

Water is essential for life on Earth. It is also what makes our planet so special. Seen from space, Earth looks like a bright blue, watery planet covered with wispy clouds. It is the only planet we currently know of with liquid water on its surface.

What is water?

Water is a tasteless, colorless, **transparent** fluid. It is found in three forms: liquid, solid, and gas. At room temperature, it is a liquid. Cool water down and it becomes solid ice. Warm it to a high temperature and it changes to an invisible gas called **water vapor**.

Water from space

Scientists believe that some of Earth's water could have come from space. Very early in Earth's history, large numbers of space rocks hit our planet. These **asteroids**, **comets**, and **meteorites** brought with them all sorts of chemicals, including those that make water.

Asteroids may have brought water when they collided with our planet billions of years ago.

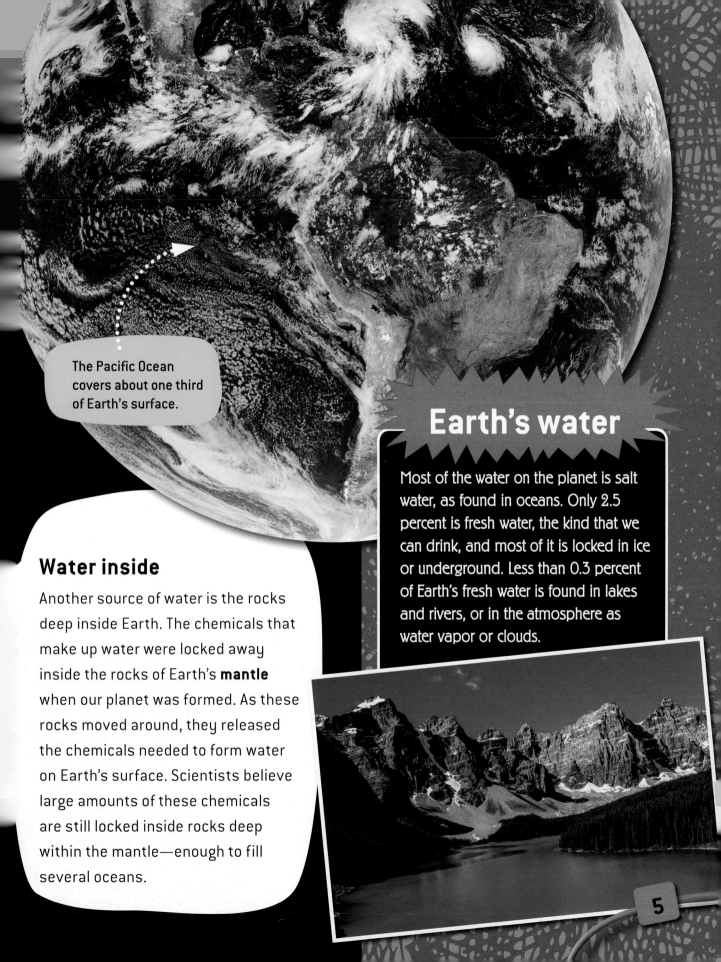

The Pacific Ocean covers about one third of Earth's surface.

Earth's water

Most of the water on the planet is salt water, as found in oceans. Only 2.5 percent is fresh water, the kind that we can drink, and most of it is locked in ice or underground. Less than 0.3 percent of Earth's fresh water is found in lakes and rivers, or in the atmosphere as water vapor or clouds.

Water inside

Another source of water is the rocks deep inside Earth. The chemicals that make up water were locked away inside the rocks of Earth's **mantle** when our planet was formed. As these rocks moved around, they released the chemicals needed to form water on Earth's surface. Scientists believe large amounts of these chemicals are still locked inside rocks deep within the mantle—enough to fill several oceans.

BRAINY BITS

The water cycle

Earth's water is constantly on the move, changing from a liquid to a gas and to a solid. The amount of water on Earth remains fairly constant. But the amount of water locked up in ice, or flowing in lakes and rivers, or carried in the atmosphere varies. The movement of water between these places, and its changes in form, is known as the water cycle.

5. Rain and snow

When the water droplets in clouds become too heavy, they fall down from the sky. If the weather is warm, they drop as rain. If it is cold, they drop as snow or **sleet**. **Hail** drops from thunder clouds.

6. Snowmelt

Snow and ice collect on the land, sometimes in glaciers high on icy, cold mountains. The glacier moves downhill and eventually the ice melts to liquid water and forms streams.

8. Reservoirs

Some streams flow into ponds and some rivers flow into lakes.

7. Run-off

Rain that has fallen flows downhill, first in streams, then in rivers. Some rainwater soaks into the ground and may emerge as **springs**.

9. Back to the sea

Eventually, the water in rivers flows back to the sea, and the cycle starts all over again.

3. Clouds

Water vapor is carried up by hot air into the atmosphere. There, it cools and changes back to its liquid form as tiny droplets of water attached to dust particles. These droplets gather together as clouds.

4. Winds

Winds blow the clouds across the ocean toward land.

Plants make the weather

Green plants have their own water cycle. Their roots take up water from the ground. The water travels up the plant to the leaves. The water then evaporates from the leaves in a process called transpiration. The water vapor rises into the atmosphere to form clouds. The clouds drop rain, which is taken up by plants, and the cycle starts again. The cycle is easy to see in tropical rainforests. The trees move so much water they actually create their own weather and cause rain showers almost every day.

2. Evaporation

Heat from the sun warms the seas and oceans. The surface water turns from liquid water to water vapor. The change is called evaporation.

1. Oceans

Most of Earth's water is in the oceans.

Water and the weather

The weather greatly depends on atmospheric pressure, which is the weight of the atmosphere pushing down on Earth's surface. Atmospheric pressure is either high or low. Hot air rises, so it creates lower air pressure than cold air, which sinks and has a high air pressure. These highs and lows move across the world, with high pressure systems delivering calm weather and low pressure systems delivering stormy weather.

Weather fronts

Weather fronts are invisible boundaries between warm and cold parts of the atmosphere. They also move along with the highs and lows. A warm front moves ahead of an area of warm air and a cold front moves in front of cold air. Most rain tends to fall just ahead of a warm front and just behind a cold front.

Clouds and weather fronts

Clouds form along weather fronts, and they appear in a certain order as the front approaches. The first signs are cirrus and stratus clouds. Next, the first altostratus and altocumulus clouds arrive, indicating the front and its rain are not far away. When cumulonimbus and giant cumulus clouds appear, the rain starts to fall.

On weather charts, a warm front is shown as a red line with semicircles, and a cold front as a blue line with triangles.

A monsoon is a weather system that drops a lot of rain on countries such as India.

Cloud spotter's guide

High-level clouds

Cirrocumulus clouds are fluffy, cotton-like cloudlets that indicate fair weather. They sometimes look like fish scales.

Cirrus clouds are wispy. One type is called mare's tails.

Mid-level clouds

Cumulonimbus is a gigantic cloud that forms from close to the ground up to 6.2 miles (10 km) in the air, and is full of energy. Watch out for thunderstorms!

Altocumulus appears as patches in settled weather, and waves when bad weather is coming.

Altostratus is a thin layer of cloud without features, but it is a sign that a storm could be on the way.

Low-level clouds

Stratocumulus is a fluffy, rounded cloud that appears in lines or waves, which can deliver light rain or snow.

Stratus is a featureless cloud that blankets everything in white or gray, and sometimes with drizzle.

Cumulus is a hill-shaped cloud. When the top is cauliflower-like, heavy showers are likely.

9

Natural water sources

When rain falls from the clouds to the ground, the ground soaks up some of the water, especially where there are many plants and trees to absorb it. The rest of the water flows downhill, first into streams and then into rivers.

Hidden water

All rainwater that seeps into the ground is called groundwater. Groundwater is less likely to be polluted than water on the surface, so it is often used for drinking water. It is either pumped up from wells or collected from natural springs. In the United States, groundwater is the largest source of fresh water. There is more of it than all the surface lakes and human-made **reservoirs** put together.

Underground water

Groundwater seeps down through the rocks and can be trapped deep below the surface in **porous** rock, in cracks, and in layers of sand, gravel, or silt.

These natural underground reservoirs are known as aquifers. Even a place as dry as the Sahara has aquifers deep below the desert. Wells can be drilled down to the aquifer and the water pumped up to supply people with fresh drinking water.

Spring water is often clean and safe to drink.

How aquifers work

Water above the more solid layer of rock flows out as streams and springs.

Trees pull up water from the ground and it evaporates from the leaves into the air.

Solid rock layer traps water below it.

A well must be drilled to get to the water below.

Natural dam

At 1,860 feet (567 m) high, the Usoi Dam in Tajikistan is the world's highest natural dam. It was not built by people, but was formed in 1911 after an earthquake caused a huge quantity of rocks to fall and block the Murghab River, creating Lake Sarez.

Water under pressure

The layers of rocks that form these aquifers might be shaped like a bowl. Water drains toward its center. If the level of the water in the sides of the bowl is above a well drilled in the center, then gravity forces water up to the surface without having to pump it. These natural bowls are called artesian basins, and the well is an artesian well.

Storing water

While nature provides many sources of water, human-made dams are also important. Dams are built across rivers, trapping water in huge artificial lakes. Huge areas of countryside are flooded behind the dam, sometimes including towns and villages.

The Mica Dam spans the Columbia River in British Columbia, Canada, and is an example of an embankment dam.

Dam design

There are several types of dams, each designed not to collapse under the weight and pressure of water behind them.

Arch dam

Made of concrete, the arch dam is curved toward the lake it holds back. It is made so that the pressure of the water behind it strengthens the dam. It is most often used across **gorges** and **canyons**.

Gravity dam

A gravity dam is made of strong materials, such as concrete and stone, which can withstand the pressure of the water behind it.

Embankment dam

Made from closely packed earth or rocks, the side facing the lake is usually lined with concrete or **masonry**. It works like a gravity dam.

The Contra Dam in Switzerland is a thin, curved arch dam.

The Hoover Dam, on the Arizona-Nevada border, is an example of a gravity dam.

Flooded wildlife

The world's largest human-made reservoir is Lake Kariba on the border of the African countries of Zambia and Zimbabwe. When the Kariba Dam was constructed, wildlife had to be rescued from the rising waters and released back into a safer area.

Weirs

Weirs or low dams are placed across rivers to restrict, or limit, but not stop the flow. Water behind the river's weir can be diverted to the water supply system.

DID YOU KNOW?

The world's highest human-made dam is the Jinping-1 Dam in China. It is 1,000 feet (305 m) high.

Electricity from water

Hydroelectric power is a by-product of storing water behind dams. It is the most widely used form of renewable **energy**, with more than 16 percent of the world's electricity generated this way.

How does it work?

The generation of **hydroelectricity** depends on **gravity**. Water from the reservoir is channeled into the power station. There, the falling or rushing water turns the propeller-like fans of a **water turbine** before the water heads out to sea. The turbine is linked to a **generator**. When the turbine turns the generator, it produces electricity. This electricity is then carried along power lines to reach the national grid.

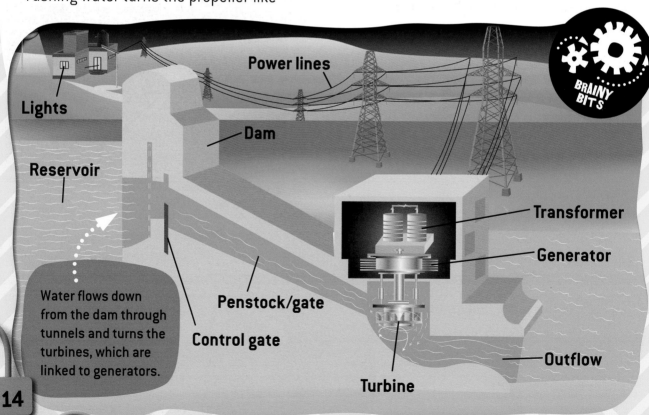

Power lines

Lights

Dam

Reservoir

BRAINY BITS

Transformer

Generator

Water flows down from the dam through tunnels and turns the turbines, which are linked to generators.

Penstock/gate

Control gate

Outflow

Turbine

14

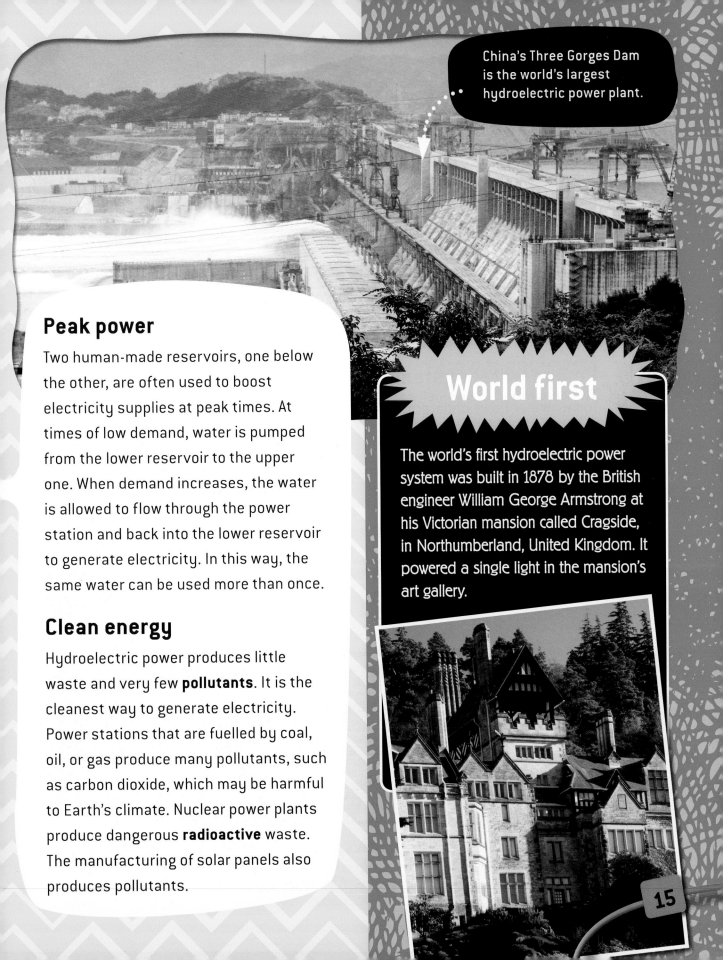

China's Three Gorges Dam is the world's largest hydroelectric power plant.

Peak power

Two human-made reservoirs, one below the other, are often used to boost electricity supplies at peak times. At times of low demand, water is pumped from the lower reservoir to the upper one. When demand increases, the water is allowed to flow through the power station and back into the lower reservoir to generate electricity. In this way, the same water can be used more than once.

Clean energy

Hydroelectric power produces little waste and very few **pollutants**. It is the cleanest way to generate electricity. Power stations that are fuelled by coal, oil, or gas produce many pollutants, such as carbon dioxide, which may be harmful to Earth's climate. Nuclear power plants produce dangerous **radioactive** waste. The manufacturing of solar panels also produces pollutants.

World first

The world's first hydroelectric power system was built in 1878 by the British engineer William George Armstrong at his Victorian mansion called Cragside, in Northumberland, United Kingdom. It powered a single light in the mansion's art gallery.

Water treatment

While underground water is safe to drink from clean wells and springs, the surface water from reservoirs, lakes, and rivers usually has to be treated before it is safe to drink. Water treatment plants can be built close to a dam, or some distance away on the outskirts of a city.

Roman water systems

Today, water flows underground in enclosed pipes, but the ancient Romans created large systems of open aqueducts, or human-made channels that carry water. The channels followed the slopes of the land, relying on water flowing downhill. Over valleys, the aqueducts were carried on special bridges. At the edge of the city, the water poured into tanks in which **sediment** settled out before the clean water flowed into households, much like modern water treatment facilities do.

Ancient Roman aqueduct Pont du Gard, near Nîmes, southern France.

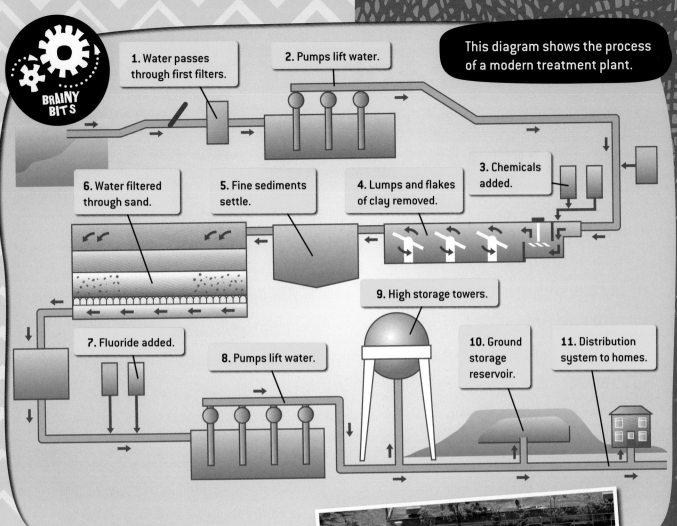

BRAINY BITS

This diagram shows the process of a modern treatment plant.

1. Water passes through first filters.

2. Pumps lift water.

3. Chemicals added.

4. Lumps and flakes of clay removed.

5. Fine sediments settle.

6. Water filtered through sand.

7. Fluoride added.

8. Pumps lift water.

9. High storage towers.

10. Ground storage reservoir.

11. Distribution system to homes.

Modern water treatment

Today, the water that flows through your household tap is treated at a water treatment plant. Gritty sediment settles in big tanks and smaller debris is filtered out. Adding chemicals such as chlorine kills **bacteria** in the water. Adding fluoride helps prevent tooth decay, especially in children. In most developed countries, treated water is pumped into towns and cities along complex networks of pipes.

Settling tanks in a water treatment plant.

DID YOU KNOW?

The word "plumber" comes from the Latin *plumbum*, meaning lead. In ancient Rome, a plumber was somebody who worked with lead.

Water for the home

Water generally reaches a home through large pipes under the street, known as water mains. Water runs through them at high pressure. Outside each house, a pressure reducer lowers the pressure before the water enters the house. This lower pressure makes sure the water comes out of the faucet at a steady rate.

Safety valve

At some point between the water main and the household supply is a special valve called a stopcock. If there is a leak in the house, the valve can be closed and the water supply cut off before any flooding occurs.

A stopcock controls the flow of water through the pipes.

Water in the house

Inside the house, cold water pipes deliver water to the faucets. When you turn the faucet on, a screw with a leather or rubber washer lifts from the end of the water pipe, allowing water to flow. When you turn it off, the screw pushes the washer down and onto the end of the water pipe, blocking the water flow.

Cold water also gets warmed in hot water tanks, which then deliver hot water to faucets. Some homes are even heated by water. Hot water is sent through ducts to heating vents or radiators in rooms throughout the house.

Water squirts up under high pressure from a burst water main.

Hard and soft water

Drinking water can be hard or soft. Its hardness depends on the rocks over which it has flowed. Hard water is found in areas with limestone and chalk. It contains high levels of the chemical calcium, which can leave a white deposit inside kitchen appliances, such as electric kettles, making them less efficient. Soft water is found where the rocks are granite or sandstone, and it does not leave a deposit. You can notice the difference between the two types of water with soap — it is much easier to make a soapy **lather** in soft water than in hard water.

Water towers

In places where the land is very flat, water is often pumped up into a large water tower, where it is stored. Pipes link the tower to homes, and gravity does the rest. It provides enough pressure to ensure the water flows freely out of the faucet.

Kuwait Water Towers are part of a modern water system built for Kuwait City.

Water at work

Water is also used outside the home. It is used in business and industry to help manufacture a wide range of products. Farming also requires a large amount of water.

When the temperature is 50 °F (10 °C) cows drink 6 gallons (23 L) of water a day — and much more when it is warmer.

Farm water

Agriculture accounts for about 70 percent of the fresh water used by people worldwide. The water is mainly used to irrigate crops. Without it, farmers would be unable to grow the food or raise the animals needed to feed the world's growing population.

Watering crops

Irrigation has been important for as long as people have been farming. At first, buckets would have been used to carry water to crops. Later civilizations, such as the ancient Egyptians, used irrigation channels. Today, all sorts of irrigation techniques are used.

In dry places, farmers have moving irrigation systems with hoses and guns on long arms that rotate around a central water supply.

Factory water

Almost every manufacturing process uses water in some way. It can be used for cooling machinery, for washing, diluting, or dissolving chemicals, and for transporting. Water can also be used within the product itself. Industries that require large quantities of water, such as paper and steel production, often have their own small, self-contained reservoirs.

Steam from cooling towers and chimneys shows how much water a factory uses.

Aquaculture

Large tanks of water are required to farm freshwater fish, such as tilapia. Farmed fish, such as trout, are bred in tanks and then released into lakes for people to catch while fishing. Farmed fish are also available for sale in local supermarkets.

A fish farm located in the countryside of Thailand.

Hydro-burgers!

Enormous quantities of water are required to make things you may not usually associate with water. A single quarter-pound hamburger, for example, requires about 540 gallons (2,044 L) of water! It takes this much water to grow the crops to feed the cattle that supply the meat for the hamburger. The cattle also have to drink and be washed, which requires more water. Overall, it takes a lot of water to make a single hamburger.

Water use in the home

Public water systems make sure that clean water reaches homes, yet only a small amount of that water is for drinking. Most is used in other household activities, such as washing and cooking.

It is important to drink plenty of water every day.

My water footprint

In countries with good water supplies, such as the U.S. and Canada, people use between 80 and 100 gallons (303 to 378 L) of water a day. If the amount of water used by agriculture and the food industry is added to this, along with all the other products we use that require water to be made, the figure rises to hundreds of billions of gallons a day in the U.S. alone.

Drinking water is used for many things other than drinking.

Where does all our water go?

Of all the clean water that is supplied to the home, only 4 percent is used as drinking water. The rest is used for household tasks, and as much as a third is just flushed away.

Personal washing 33%

Toilet flushing 30%

Clothes washing 13%

Watering the garden and washing the car 7%

Washing dishes 8%

Other uses 5%

Add up your average daily water consumption

Copy this water consumption chart onto a piece of paper.

Fill it in every day and add up how much water you use in a week.

Daily activity	Average water consumed per use	Uses per week	x No. of people in household	Weekly total
Bath	36 gallons (136 L)	x ⬭	x ⬭	= ⬭
20 minute shower	40 gallons (151 L)	x ⬭	x ⬭	= ⬭
10 minute shower	20 gallons (75.7 L)	x ⬭	x ⬭	= ⬭
Toilet flush	3 gallons (11.35 L)	x ⬭	x ⬭	= ⬭
Brushing teeth*	1 gallon (3.78L)	x ⬭	x ⬭	= ⬭
Hand/face wash	1 gallon (3.78 L)	x ⬭	x ⬭	= ⬭

*with tap running

Daily activity	Average water consumed per use	Uses per week	Weekly total
Washing machine	30 gallons (113.5 L)	x ⬭	= ⬭
Dishwasher	26 gallons (98 L)	x ⬭	= ⬭
Food preparation	4 gallons (15 L)	x ⬭	= ⬭
Hand-washing dishes	25 gallons (94.6 L)	x ⬭	= ⬭

Total use of water by your household	= ⬭

Divide by 7 for daily consumption	= ⬭
Divide by number of people to find each person's average	= ⬭
Add 8 gallons (30 L) for miscellaneous water uses	= ⬭

Total average daily water consumption per person	= ⬭

How does your daily water consumption compare with the 80 to 100 gallons (303 to 378 L) per person national average?

23

How to save water

People in countries with good water supplies tend to take water for granted. They turn on the tap and out it flows. This can lead to waste. Water can be wasted in all sorts of ways, from damaged water mains to leaks in the system. However, a lot of water waste can be avoided by people being careful about how much they use.

Here are some tips...

- Turn off the tap when brushing your teeth. It wastes more than 1.5 gallons (6 L) per minute.

- Fix a dripping tap. It can waste about 15 gallons (57 L) of water a week.

- Shorter showers, about 4 minutes, are less wasteful than baths. A bath uses about 36 gallons (136 L) of water, while a shower uses a third of that.

- New modern toilets are designed to use less water per flush.

- Fill a jug with water and place it in the fridge so you won't have to run the tap to get a cold drink.

- Fill cooking pots and kettles with only the amount of water needed.

> Always make sure a dishwasher or washing machine is full before starting it. Choose the economy or eco-option cycle.

- Wash fruit and vegetables in a bowl, not under running water.

- Water the garden with a watering can, not a hose, and water in the early morning or evening.

- Check the water bill or water meter for usage. Knowing the exact amount of water you use, and how much is being paid for it, might encourage you not to waste it.

Free water

One way to save water is to have your own mini-reservoir. You can collect rainwater by using a rain barrel that is fed by the gutter that carries water off the roof of your house.

Remember to turn the tap off while brushing your teeth.

DID YOU KNOW?

In hot, dry weather, up to half of the water used per person is actually used on gardens and lawns!

Drinking water

People need to drink clean water to live healthy lives. Water flushes out dangerous chemicals from your body's organs, carries nutrients to your cells, and generally helps keep your body working properly. A lack of water can lead to dehydration.

Water for health

It is often said that a healthy person should drink about eight glasses of water per day, but no single formula fits everybody. Even so, health authorities suggest that a half gallon (2 L) of fluids a day, including water and other beverages, is beneficial.

Active people

Children who do activities such as team sports need more water to replace the water lost through sweating. Active people in hot countries also need more water, up to 4 gallons (15 L) a day in extreme cases.

Clean, fresh water is essential for good health.

People who are active need to drink water more regularly.

About 65 percent of the human body is water. A newborn baby can be as much as 75 percent water, while an elderly person can be as little as 45 percent water.

Where does our body water come from?

Drinking water and other beverages, including tea and coffee, accounts for 75 percent of our daily water intake. We can also get water from food. The water content of different foods varies, but on average, 25 percent of our water intake comes from food.

Butter
15
percent
water

Tomato
94
percent
water

Bread
35
percent
water

Milk
87
percent
water

Boiled egg
73
percent
water

Tea and coffee
99
percent
water

Clean water for everyone

There are more than seven billion people in the world, of which one billion have no access to clean drinking water. Two million die every year from diseases contracted through contaminated water.

Drinking water from the sea

Desalination is the process of removing salt from salt water to make fresh water. With droughts more likely in the future, desalination could help with water shortages, but it requires a lot of electricity. In Europe, it is used to top up water supplies, but in the Middle East, many countries depend on it.

The good news

In 2000, the United Nations asked all its members to cut in half the number of people who do not have clean water by 2015. This was achieved five years early, when over two billion more people had clean drinking water in 2010 than in 1990.

The bad news

Although nearly 90 percent of people worldwide have access to clean drinking water, this leaves more than 10 percent who do not. Many live in areas without water systems or **sewers**. They collect their water from open pits and ponds, and it can be contaminated by sewage. Terrible diseases, such as **cholera**, are common.

This man's only water supply is a dirty river.

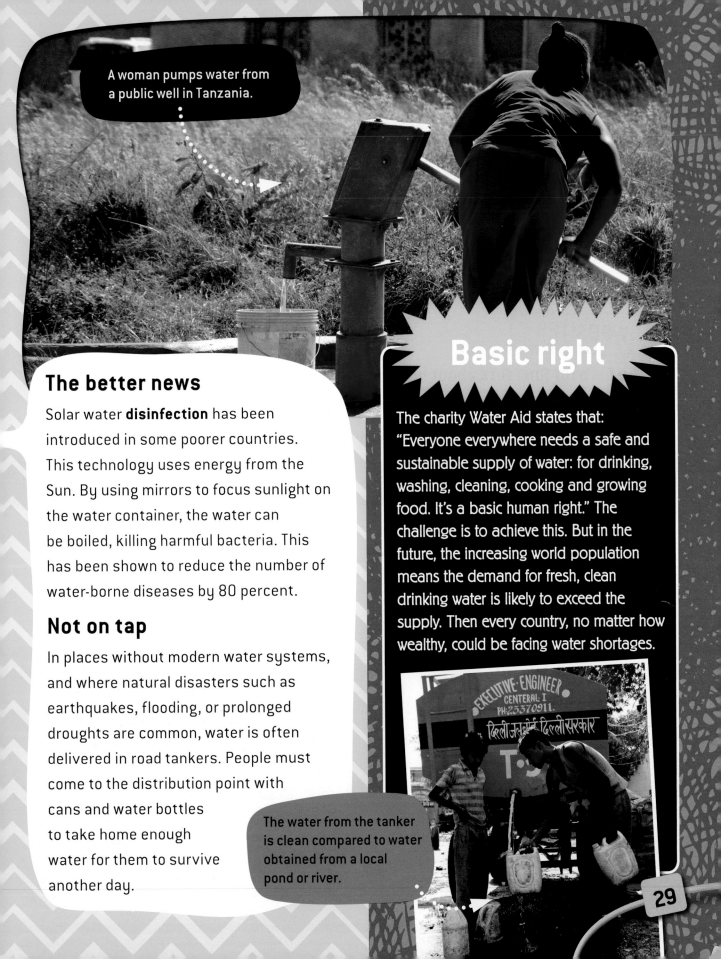

A woman pumps water from a public well in Tanzania.

Basic right

The charity Water Aid states that: "Everyone everywhere needs a safe and sustainable supply of water: for drinking, washing, cleaning, cooking and growing food. It's a basic human right." The challenge is to achieve this. But in the future, the increasing world population means the demand for fresh, clean drinking water is likely to exceed the supply. Then every country, no matter how wealthy, could be facing water shortages.

The better news

Solar water **disinfection** has been introduced in some poorer countries. This technology uses energy from the Sun. By using mirrors to focus sunlight on the water container, the water can be boiled, killing harmful bacteria. This has been shown to reduce the number of water-borne diseases by 80 percent.

Not on tap

In places without modern water systems, and where natural disasters such as earthquakes, flooding, or prolonged droughts are common, water is often delivered in road tankers. People must come to the distribution point with cans and water bottles to take home enough water for them to survive another day.

The water from the tanker is clean compared to water obtained from a local pond or river.

Further information

BOOKS

Earth's Water Cycle by Diane Dakers, Crabtree Publishing, 2016

Hydroelectric Power: Power from Moving Water by Marguerite Rodger, Crabtree Publishing, 2010

Save Water by Kay Barnham, Crabtree Publishing, 2008

Water Supply: Can the Earth Cope? by Louise Spilsbury, Wayland, 2013

WEBSITES

Go here for fun facts about how to save water:
www3.epa.gov/watersense/kids

This webpage will give you a lot of information about water energy:
www.eia.gov/kids/energy.cfm?page=hydropower_home-basics-k.cfm

Test your water knowledge with this fun quiz:
www.kids.nationalgeographic.com/kids/games/puzzlesquizzes/water-wiz/

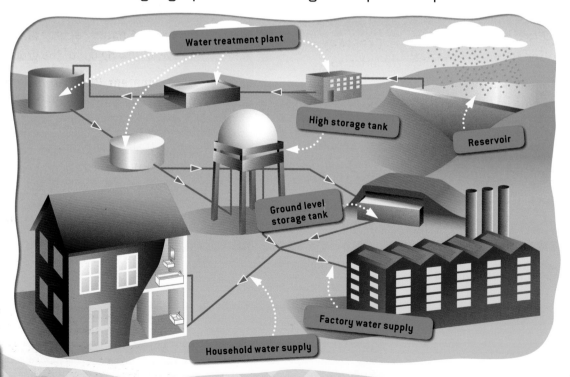

Glossary

asteroid A small, rocky object that orbits the Sun

atmosphere The layer of gases surrounding Earth

atmospheric pressure The pressure exerted by the weight of air in the atmosphere

bacteria Tiny, microscopic life forms that can cause disease

canyon A narrow valley with steep cliff walls

cholera A dangerous disease of the small intestine caused by bacteria, often found in dirty water

comet A small space object of ice and dust that sometimes has a "tail" of gas and dust particles when near the Sun

contaminate To make something impure with a pollutant

dehydration The huge loss of water from the body

disinfect To cleanse something and kill any bacteria in it

generator A machine that makes electricity

gorge A deep, narrow valley with very steep sides

gravity The force that causes objects to fall to the ground or water to flow downhill

hail Falling pellets of ice

hydroelectricity Electricity generated using the movement of water

irrigation Supplying water to farmland by sprinklers, ditches, or channels

lather A foam made with soap and water

mantle The layer of Earth between the central core and the outer crust

masonry Stonework or brickwork

meteorite A stony or metallic object that falls to Earth from outer space

pollutant A waste product that makes air or water dirty and not suitable or safe to use

porous Describes something that allows the passage of gases and liquids, such as a sponge

radioactive Describes something that gives off dangerous rays

renewable Describes something that never runs out

reservoir A place where large amounts of fluid collects

sediment A material that settles to the bottom of a liquid

sewer A drain or pipe that takes away waste water from the house and rainwater from the street

sleet Pellets of melting snowflakes or freezing raindrops

spring A natural source of water flowing out of the ground

transparent Describes objects that can be seen through

water turbine A machine with a propellor-like wheel that is turned by the movement of water

water vapor The gas phase of water

Index

A

agriculture 20, 22
aqueducts 16
aquifers 10, 11
artesian basins 11
artesian wells 11
atmosphere 5, 6, 7, 8

C, D

climate 15
clouds 4, 5, 6, 7, 8, 9, 10
dams 11, 12, 13, 14, 15, 16
dehydration 26
desalination 28

E

electricity 14–15, 28
evaporation 7, 11

F, G

farming 20, 21
food industry 22
groundwater 10

H, I, O

hydroelectricity 14, 15
irrigation 20
oceans 5, 7

R

rainwater 10, 25
renewable energy 14
reservoirs 6, 10, 13, 14, 15, 16, 21
rivers 5, 6, 10, 11, 12, 13, 16, 28, 29

T, W

transpiration 7
water treatment plants 16–17
water cycle 6–7
weather systems 8